Copyright © 2019 by Jenny Weaver Worships, LLC

Visit our website:

www.JennyWeaverWorships.com

Printed in the United States of America. All rights reserved under International Copyright Law. Contents and/or cover may not be reproduced in whole or in part.

Cover Design: Christopher Negron
Interior Design: Stacy Riddle

Rev 010420

Jenny Weaver
WORSHIPS

Jenny Weaver is an amazing wife, mother, author, teacher, and Holy Ghost filled worshipper of God. She believes in building families and communities in the Kingdom of God. She is best known for **"Singing the Scriptures"** live on Facebook and other social media platforms. She reaches the nations with a heart of worship postured towards the King, and in turn, the King postures His heart towards the nations, through her, bringing healing and joy to the people. Countless testimonies come in daily sharing how their lives have been completely changed since watching Jenny sing the scriptures.

Once a homeless, drug addict and self-cutting Wiccan, Jenny is now a true Prophetic worshipper and lover of God. Transformed by His renewing power, Jenny's heart is to continue to lead people into an encounter with the Holy Spirit that will posture them in the direction of transformation and restoration. She now reaches the nations and mentors countless lives all over the world on how to lead with spiritual authority.

Her inspirational testimony has been featured by networks all over the world such as the Word Network, TBN's Sid Roth - It's Supernatural, and Life Today with James and Betty Robison. Her first official hard copy book printed with Destiny Image Publishing entitled, **'The Sound of Freedom'** hit shelves in 2019. In the establishment of the **JW Online Academy** many other books and e-books have followed since. She has a passion for teaching and leaves the people in a state of constant overflow by being obedient to the direction of God. She works closely with Compassion International to help bring restoration to children all around the world.

Jenny believes that worship, led in Spirit and in Truth, with a pure heart and no limitations, ushers in the Glory of God; this, in turn, invades the earth! It is Jenny's desire to continue to lead **prophetic and spontaneous, high praise worship** that releases the song of the LORD into the Hearts of the people and children all over the world.

"I am amazed at the hand of God on my life."
- Jenny Weaver

INTRODUCTION

I remember sitting in a church service years ago, my mind wandering, unfocused on the service, thinking on the things I was tasked to do for the coming week. All of a sudden, I realized I was getting nothing out of the service. I looked around and saw the faces of the people, bored and unengaged. Some were nodding off; some looking at their phones; and I thought to myself, "*there must be more than this?*"

In that moment, I determined in my heart to seek more of God, desiring to experience the exciting, power filled life I read about in the bible. I read about the first Apostles healing the sick, casting out devils, and leading thousands, upon thousands to the LORD. I longed for a life like that! I knew in my heart that, if I wanted this, it was time to advance in the things of God. Yes, I was saved; I attended church and occasionally read my bible. I prayed over my food and sang a few worship songs, every now and then. Still, I felt I wasn't living the life that Christ intended for me to live; the one He gave His life for. I was comfortable and complacent and, what seemed like out of nowhere, I wanted more! At this point, some of you might be saying, "I completely relate to this", because you've accepted and committed yourself to this invitation to **Level Up** in your walk with the LORD.

So, I invite you to dine with the LORD and lean into Him. He wants to take you higher in the things of God. I can tell you that, when I began to seek him, I found more and more of Him. I came into new, amazing levels of God and I am still finding more and more of him every day. Your hunger is about to be stirred in such a personal way; so, get ready! It's time to Level Up and come into the fullness of God.

I am excited to be on this journey with you. It is my prayer that the next 21 days will show as a new season for you and prove to be unforgettable; forever shifting and transforming your walk with Him!

PRACTICAL APPLICATION

The beauty of the JW Online Academy is it is designed to present different ways to walk out your time learning with the LORD. It is your choice on how you would like to walk it out. This flexibility opens the door for a more lasting commitment and sets you up for success on your journey. I have highlighted three main ways below to give you a starting point along with the study of the month. You can certainly go at your own pace; set aside a certain time with the LORD every day as you walk out the 21-Day journey.

The 4-Week Study

This option serves as a great weekday option with a time of rest during the weekend. It is designed to approach this with five days on and two days off to review and reflect.

Mon – Fri: Study the Devotion of the Day.

Sat – Sun: Rest & Reflect on the scriptures and the material covered throughout the week, put it into practice.

21-Day Study

This option serves as an amazing devotional to couple with a **21-Day Fast** of your choice.

Days 1-20:   20 Daily Lessons coupled with Prayer and Fasting.

Day 21:   **Final Thoughts**: Rest & Reflect on your time of learning, fasting & praying. Identify breakthroughs and challenges to overcome and make preparations to *exit the fast in excellence.*

Go at Your Own Pace:

This is ideal for those of you on the go or with limited time. It is geared to work with your specific schedule or group with **no time restraint.**

Webinar of the Month:

JW Online Academy Members Only: In addition to the daily video lessons, once a month there will be a live webinar on the JW Academy Members Facebook Page with Q&A on the study of the month.

TABLE OF CONTENTS

Week One

Day 01	Having a Made-Up Mind
Day 02	Find Your Place
Day 03	Set A Time
Day 04	Establish Truth
Day 05	Be Still

Week Two

Day 06	Be Led by the Spirit
Day 07	An All-Day Affair
Day 08	Soak it Up
Day 09	Consecrate
Day 10	Communion

Week Three

Day 11	Pray in the Spirit
Day 12	A Heart Check
Day 13	No Shame
Day 14	A Jesus Centered Life
Day 15	Desire

Week Four

Day 16	Oil Up
Day 17	Your Tongue
Day 18	Time to Submit
Day 19	Children's Bread
Day 20	Come Up
Day 21	Rest & Reflect - Final Thoughts

Day One **A MADE UP MIND**

Are you ready to get started? I know you are, because you are here; you have a desire on the inside of you to grow your walk in the LORD.

There is a saying, "you can WANT to do something; you can TRY to do something, but it isn't until you DECIDE to do something that things happen and begin to steer you in the direction you desire." I want you to have "A Made-Up Mind'. Determine and decide today that you will succeed, and you will complete what you start. If you are like me, you may have high hopes of starting a new project or class, but, after a few days, lack the zeal and desire that was there in the beginning. This is where most people give up and say, "oh well, forget it". We are changing that today! I want you to purpose in your heart that you will stick this out and see it all the way through to completion!

I am going to give you 20 days' worth of tips, teaching, and practical tools that I have found to be key in going to new, greater levels in your walk with God; in turn, you will be making your entire life blessed, fruitful, productive and filled with power and love!

I want to encourage you and let you know that I am cheering you on! That God, the Father, Jesus, the Holy Spirit, and all of heaven wants you to see this through so that you can start living that abundant life Jesus paid so dearly for you to have.

SCRIPTURE FOCUS

Psalms 51:10 (PAR) Create in me a pure heart, o God, and renew a steadfast spirit within me.

Have you ever thought about the word 'steadfast'? Well let's take a look...

sted-fast -adj.
Fixed in a direction; firmly in place, immovable, not subject to change, firm in belief, determination, loyal and faithful.

Wow! That is what we need when it comes to spending time with God daily. We need that kind of steadfast, made-up mind where we are unmoved by all that goes on around us.

So, in the past, if you have struggled with spending time daily in the Word and worshipping Him, today the slate is clean. Decide to have a Made-Up Mind" to devote time to Him every day!

ASSIGNMENT

Today, SURRENDER all those old habits of starting something and not finishing it. Forgive yourself and move forward.

PRAYER

Father,

Thank you for another amazing day to draw closer to you. I surrender all my old habits, ways of thinking and responses to you now. I declare that I have your power living on the inside of me to complete what I start, and I cannot fail! I receive all you have for me and I make up my mind to devote my life, time, wants, and my will to you today and forever more. Help me where I am weak, and I thank you in advance.

In Jesus Mighty Name, Amen

※ Day One **A MADE UP MIND**

Psalms 51:10 Create in me a pure heart, o God, and renew a steadfast spirit within me

Day Two **FIND YOUR PLACE**

Let's face it, life gets busy! Every day we have a million things on our to-do list that seems to consume our day and, by the time you realize that you need to read your word or spend time with God, you are exhausted and just ready to call it a day. So, today, we are going to discuss finding a designated time and place that you can go to every day to be alone with Jesus.

Resist the temptation to get overly complicated with this or you can find yourself heading down a road to failure. Rather, find a secret place that you can meet with the King. A space that is quiet, comfortable, neat, and distraction free.

Psalms 91:1 (KJV) He who dwells in the secret place of the Most High shall abide in the shadow of the Almighty.

My first 'place' was our old RV parked in the back of the house. I would get up every day and, sometimes at night as well, and walk into our backyard with coffee in hand to spend time alone with God; place where I could pour out to Him and He pour into me.

When the family would travel, my 'place' would become our car. Before anyone would get up, I would get into the car, turn on some worship music, grab my bible, and just simply sit with the LORD. Even if I was only able to carve out five or ten minutes, one thing was sure: my day started with Him (and a little coffee)!

You may have a space in your closet, a writing desk, or a spare room that you can make your 'place'; whatever it is, purpose in your heart to meet with the LORD there every day and this will push you towards discovering the great things of God.

SCRIPTURE FOCUS

Mark 1:35 (KJV) And in the morning, rising up a great while before day, He went out, and departed into a solitary place, and there He prayed.

Take note: Going to a solitary place was a habit for Jesus, not a chore! He made it a point every day to get alone with God. He received insight, revelation and fellowship with the Father and Holy Spirit by doing this. If Jesus had to get alone with God daily, how much more do we need to do this? Friends, find that special place where you and the LORD can commune and fellowship together.

ASSIGNMENT

Find your place! Grab your bible, pens, paper, journal, rug (for some floor time), music player and anything else that will make this your special place.

PRAYER

Father,

I love you and I thank you for this amazing day where I get to fellowship with you and learn more about your love for me. Help me find this place just for us. I consecrate it to you. May it be a place where we create the most amazing memories in. Lead and guide me today in all your ways. I pray that I walk in your Spirit everywhere my feet trod.

In Jesus Mighty Name, Amen

Day Two **FIND YOUR PLACE**

Psalms 91:1
He who dwells in the secret place of the Most High
shall abide in the shadow of the Almighty

Day Three SET A TIME

I am a wife and a home school mom. We have two dogs, full schedules, and a lot going on from day to day. Being a traveling minister, running an online shop & school, managing nine social media platforms, taking care of a house, and a whole lot of other people can prove to be a lot most days. If I am not careful, the day will get rolling full steam ahead until night falls. I have made up my mind that my time with the LORD is in those first morning hours of the day before anyone is up and moving.

I used to hate getting up early so my devotion time was at night. Once my schedule became full, I would find myself falling asleep while reading the word or dosing off while worshiping God. Then, there were times when my family would come to me with things they needed, and I became distracted.

I felt the LORD prompting me to get up in the early morning hours. I told the LORD, "if this is what you really want, I will say yes, but please give me the strength and desire to get up early with you every day." Guess what? He did! I would set my alarm and find myself wide awake a few minutes before my alarm even went off. That was nothing but the LORD; TRUST ME!!

SCRIPTURE FOCUS

Matthew 6:33 (KJV) But rather seek ye the Kingdom of God, and all these things shall be added unto you.

Your life and schedule may not be a perfect fit for the morning hours and that's okay but find a time and set it. I challenge you to start your day off with time alone with Jesus. You may not feel like it; you may feel weary or you're just going through a lot, but I promise you, it is not time wasted. You may go in tired, but you will come out energized with power and joy. It WILL be worth it!

SET IT: DON'T FORGET IT!

ASSIGNMENT

Write in the comments or notes the time you and LORD have decided on to meet.

*Set THREE alarms on your phone as a reminder to pray throughout the day.

PRAYER

Father,

I come to you today and I lift your Holy name. Thank you for all you have done, all you are doing, and all the things you plan to do in my life. I am setting this time aside for us so that I may get to know you more Father. I know that in doing this you will meet me in such a mighty and powerful way. I ask that you cover me today. Thank you that you go before me and burn up all my enemies.

In Jesus Mighty Name, Amen

Day Three **SET A TIME**

Matthew 6:33
But rather seek ye the Kingdom of God,
and all these things shall be added unto you

Day Four ESTABLISH TRUTH

How are you going to be strong in your devotion time, your walk with the LORD, and be impactful in the world we live in? We do it by knowing His truth! Sounds simple, I know, but we must truly know the truth of the gospel and have sound doctrine to walk out the destiny God has for us. Without His truth, we won't stay constant in devotion; it's that simple.

So, now that we know it's His truth, we need to come and dismantle all of Satan's lies and the doctrine of this world, the lust of the flesh, to get it and to know it!

Today, we focus on God's truth over everything!

SCRIPTURE FOCUS

John 8:32 (NIV) Then you will know the TRUTH, and the TRUTH will set you free.

This is a popular verse, and I am sure you have it memorized, but I want you to look closely at it today. Notice it says, "you will *know* the truth." Once you know the truth, it is that truth that will set you free. "What is truth?" Or should I say, "Who is Truth?" This scripture is pointing us to know Jesus. The bible says that Jesus is the truth and the Holy Spirit is the Spirit of Truth. To be set free and walk in total victory, we must 'know' the LORD. It's not enough to have just simply heard about him, we must KNOW Him in a very deep and personal way.

Jesus brings us into a revelation of Truth that comes from His presence and it can transform and completely change us from the inside out. That is why this scripture speaks of us being set free; free from the lies of the enemy, free from the past, free from sin, free from hurt, and free from bondage in Jesus name.

ASSIGNMENT

Search out a few scriptures on TRUTH and meditate on them today. Write one of them down in your journal.

PRAYER

Father,

I thank you for your TRUTH in my life. I ask you, Spirit of Truth, to come and dismantle the lies of the enemy! I receive the Truth of your word LORD; teach me how to discern the Truth from a lie. I praise you, today, and give all the Glory and honor.

In Jesus Mighty Name, Amen

Day Four ESTABLISH TRUTH

John 8:32
**Then you will know the TRUTH,
and the TRUTH will set you free**

Day Five **BE STILL**

One of the most important things I do when I am spending time with the LORD is that I make it a point to *pause to listen*. I used to fill my devotion time up with a lot of chatter, singing, talking, praying, crying, and several other things, but the LORD has taught me to be quiet in his presence and listen.

This is something you must train yourself to do, because it doesn't feel natural at first. Even when we look at our corporate gatherings, we don't normally see parts of the service with everything and everyone completely silent, so we can hear from the LORD. In fact, it would probably feel very awkward if that happened on a Sunday morning! If you want the most out of your walk with the LORD and desire going deeper into the things of God, then you must learn to pause and listen and put it into practice.

SCRIPTURE FOCUS

Psalms 46:10 (KJV) Be Still and know that I am God: I will be exalted among the heathen; I will be exalted in the earth.

Have you ever thought your spouse wasn't listening to you? I'm guessing it bothered you a little bit, right? Or maybe it bothered you a lot, because you were pouring your heart out. For a relationship to grow and be strong, both people must learn the art of listening and communicating in a healthy way. It's no different with the LORD. He has things He wants to say to us as much as we have things, we want to say to Him. Quiet your spirit and be still so that you can hear the LORD and begin to truly know the truth.

When I first started doing this, my flesh went crazy! I had a million things flood my mind. I was antsy and could not sit still for a long period of time. During this time of me being still and listening, my flesh was dying and putting up a fight. I learned to push past that until I was completely still in my heart, mind, body, and spirit before the LORD. Once that happened, I was able to hear revelation, instruction, and the voice of the Father clearly. Your entire walk with the LORD will shift if you master this.

ASSIGNMENT

Sit still and wait upon the LORD. Start at about 5-10 minutes sitting before the LORD during devotion and prepare your spirit to hear from Him. Do this daily and increase the time after a week.

PRAYER

Father,

I come before you to sit in your presence and be still just to know you more. LORD, help me to quiet the noise of life and solely tune my spiritual ears to hear from you, today. I know you are speaking, and I will position myself to receive from you, today.

In Jesus Mighty Name, Amen

Day Five **BE STILL**

Psalms 46:10
Be Still and know that I am God:
I will be exalted among the heathen;
I will be exalted in the earth

Day Six **BE LED BY THE SPIRIT**

Religion, tradition, and rituals can cause the Spirit of God to go silent in our lives if we are not careful! Many people fall into a trap of dead, dry religion. They have no idea that they are not being led by the Spirit, because they are used to doing the same things over and over, like a check list of sorts that they deem right before the LORD.

Jesus was led by the Spirit of God in everything He did! Notice, His ministry and life were not boring or dry. It was powerful, full of life, exciting, life changing, something fresh and new. He was led by the Spirit.

As you commit yourself to the LORD and want to go deeper in the things of God, you must shake off any old patterns of a religious mindset; that kind of mindset says, "this is how I've always done it, so I won't change" or "I've never seen that before, so it can't be God". Now, I fully believe in using discernment, but, if I see something I haven't seen before, I ask the Holy Spirit, "Is this you?" If it is, I ask Him to teach me how to embrace it. I never want to say something isn't God if it is Him and I'm just not used to the way He is moving.

SCRIPTURE FOCUS

Romans 8:14 (NIV) For those who are Led by the Spirit of God are the Children of God.

During your devotion time with the LORD, He may lead you to do something completely different than what you planned or expected; but follow Him. He may have you lay on your face and cry out in the Spirit for an hour, write a love letter, or pray for someone you don't even know; whatever it is, follow Him. Listen to that still, small voice.

The scripture tells us plainly that only those who are led by the Spirit are truly his children. Meaning, if you are not Spirit led, you are not His child. Today is a great day to make a commitment to be led by His Spirit from this day forward.

ASSIGNMENT

Think of five areas you want the Spirit of God to take over and write them out. Begin to invite His Spirit to lead you in those areas now. Focus on His voice during the day.

PRAYER

Father,

I love you and I thank you that your Spirit is leading and guiding me in your truth. Help me to surrender every area of my life to the leading of your Spirit. If there are areas that I have not fully given to you, I repent of it now and I release them to you.

In Jesus Mighty Name, Amen

Day Six BE LED BY THE SPIRIT

Romans 8:14
For those who are Led by the Spirit of God
are the Children of God

Day Seven AN ALL-DAY AFFAIR

Over the years, I have found, if we are not careful, we can tend to put limitations on our time of devotion with the LORD. Most will try to 'fit' Him into their day versus 'fit' their day into Him and all that He has for us to receive. He wants to give us a gift of impartation. When we limit our time with Him, we miss out on these priceless moments.

The heart of the LORD is calling us to break out of this box of limitation we tend to put Him in. Believe it or not, He doesn't just want minimal time with us every day! He wants a constant and never-ending fellowship! After all, we are His temple; we are His house and dwelling place.

I remember just starting out in my Faith walk with the LORD. I had this misconception that God stayed within this 'morning bubble' and that was it. Oh, but when I discovered the joys of communing with Him all throughout the day, *my life completely SHIFTED!*

I want to challenge you to take Jesus out of this box of limitation and let Him have free reign, all day, in every area of your life. Make it an All-Day Affair for He cares for you! He cares about your stay at home mom things, your career, your marriage, your friendships, your desires, your well-being, your health, and every area of your life – yes, He wants all of you!

SCRIPTURE FOCUS
Psalms 34:1 (ASV) I will bless Jehovah at all times: His praise shall continually be in my mouth.

Have you ever felt guilty for not spending enough time with the LORD? Have you had something come up and you were not able to get into your 'secret place' and felt conviction later? Most likely, your answer is yes. God calls us to renew our mind daily.

Praying a few minutes here and there, all throughout the day, is one way you can break that spirit of condemnation off your life. Praying in your prayer language is another amazing tool to renew your mind and declare that Spirit of Praise over you. This opens up your communication with your Heavenly Father all throughout the day, causing you to posture your heart to towards Him, and readies you for any instruction or revelation that He may impart to you.

This is not as hard as it may seem; to pray all day; to give God praise all day, in all things. We should be thinking on Him and giving Him thanks for even the small things. The things that may seem insignificant are important to Him. The LORD loves those who are thankful and mindful of Him.

ASSIGNMENT
Start taking breaks throughout your day to pray; when you are getting ready for the day, your morning commute, on a break or lunch, or cooking dinner. Take intentional time during the day to meet with the LORD.

PRAYER
Father,

I thank you for this day and I thank you, God, that you are always available to me. I lean into you and ask you to help me, LORD, to exalt you, praise you, and lift your name up all throughout my day. I make it a point to find intentional time with you. I declare this is your day; a day you have made, and I rejoice and am glad in it.

In Jesus Mighty Name, Amen

Day Seven **AN ALL-DAY AFFAIR**

Psalms 34:1
I will bless Jehovah at all times:
His praise shall continually be in my mouth

Day Eight **SOAK IT UP**

Soaking is one of my favorite things to do! If you don't know what soaking is, I will explain. Soaking is simply resting in the presence of God, meditating on Him and Him alone. It's where His power and presence are revealed and really begins to transform you from the inside out!

Many times, we lean towards doing spiritual warfare as our primary goal in our prayer time with the LORD, and I agree, there is certainly a time and a place for that! It is important to remember we must maintain balance! If we spend all of our prayer time focused on binding up the devil, we will have missed valuable opportunities to just be in the presence of God, which will lead us down a path that ends in frustration and hopelessness.

SCRIPTURE FOCUS
Psalms 23:5 (ASV) Thou hast anointed my head with oil; My cup runneth over.

Imagine you had a dry rag and a bucket of water or oil. If you were to take that dry rag and dunk it all the way in the bucket, it would come out completely drenched and saturated. Even if you tried to ring it out, it would still be drenched and saturated with liquid; that is the idea behind soaking! It is in this place; you get so wrapped up in God's presence that you come out covered from head to toe with His precious Spirit. With a precious oil and fragrance that says, "I've been with the King" and, no matter what, you are still going to have His presence and glory all over you; this will help you navigate anything that comes your way!

Sometimes, life can bring us to a state of exhaustion. With all the things on our to-do list and trying to be as effective as we can, sometimes we just need the 'Rest of God' to come upon us so that we can breathe again. Put all our cares at His feet and just focus our attention on the goodness of God and how amazing Jesus is. During this time for me, I lay down, worship music playing softly, singing quietly sometimes, meditating and gazing on His beauty. I focus my thoughts towards the 'person' of Jesus until that picture becomes very clear in my spirit.

Soaking prepares you for busy days where you may not have much time. I challenge you to implement this in your daily devotion time every now and then, or as much as you like! Get ready to discover a deeper intimacy with the LORD in this place.

ASSIGNMENT
It is time to SOAK! Set aside 20-30 minutes to soak in His presence. Have a paper and pen nearby, just in case you hear a word of the LORD being spoken to you.

PRAYER
Father,

I come to you today, just to gaze upon you and magnify your name! You are worthy of every bit of my praise and worship. I want to see you face to face and encounter you. I want to see you like you really are; high and lifted up! You are my everything, LORD. Help me soak in all you are and all you have for me, today.

In Jesus Mighty Name, Amen

Day Eight **SOAK IT UP**

Level Up

Psalms 23:5
Thou hast anointed my head with oil; My cup runneth over

Day Nine CONSECRATE

con-se-cra-tion —noun
the action of making or declaring something sacred. To set apart for a special use.

I believe consecration is a lost art in the church as a whole. Jesus lived the greatest example of a consecrated life, that of fasting and prayer. The word of God tells us that Jesus is also God and came to earth as a man. It amazes me that Jesus, even though He is God in the flesh, still had to fast and consecrate Himself unto the Father. Jesus knew the power of pushing fleshly desires aside and getting His eyes fixed on His Heavenly Father.

When Jesus was led into the wilderness, He was not led there by the devil. The Bible shows us, in Luke chapter four, that the Spirit of God led Him into the wilderness to fast for forty days and nights.

If Jesus had to fast and live a consecrated life, we certainly should be fasting and living our lives consecrated and sold out for God! When you consecrate yourself to the LORD, it's a very special thing and seen as a serious act of worship.

SCRIPTURE FOCUS
Joshua 3:5 (NIV) Then Joshua told the people, "Consecrate yourselves, for tomorrow the LORD will do amazing things among you."

What consecration looks like for me in my everyday life, sometimes I am led to fast from sun-up to sun-down and focus my mind on prayer during that time. Other times, I will set aside a few hours to hear from the LORD and pour myself out unto Him; no distractions. At times, I break from social media or other things to free up time to focus on the LORD. This process may look completely different for you, but make it a point to purpose in your heart to consecrate yourself unto the LORD and He will do amazing things among you!

ASSIGNMENT
Plan out a time of consecration and mark it on the calendar. If you mess up, don't get fed up – Try again. No condemnation!

PRAYER
Father,

My entire life belongs to you. I love you with all of me and I consecrate myself to you; not just today, but every day. I am yours and you are mine! Help me to push aside fleshly desires and the pleasures of this world to go after all I have in you.

In Jesus Mighty Name, Amen

Day Nine CONSECRATE

Level Up

Joshua 3:5
Then Joshua told the people, "Consecrate yourselves, for tomorrow the LORD will do <u>amazing things</u> among you."

Day Ten COMMUNION

Com-mun-ion –noun
1. *The sharing or exchanging of intimate thoughts and feelings, especially when the exchange is on a mental or spiritual level.*
2. *The service of Christian worship at which bread and wine are consecrated and shared.*

I am going to discuss the topic of Communion today, specifically the meaning of communion, and how it can serve you and prepare you for things to come.

There is a great amount of power in both of the meanings listed above. Most people think communion is something you do every now and then during church, where you partake in a little cracker and grape juice, but it is far more significant than that!

Communion is significant, because it is a Holy time of worship when we corporately come together as one body to remember and celebrate what Christ did for us. When we are consecrating ourselves before the LORD in our secret place, it is an act of obedience unto the LORD; it is a time of examination to hear from the LORD on all areas of our life.

I want you to begin to implement both sharing & exchanging of intimate thoughts and feelings along with a show of worship during your time of devotion. Begin a healthy habit of remembering Him on a very regular basis, not just once or twice a year.

SCRIPTURE FOCUS

Luke 22: 19-20 (NIV) And He took bread, gave thanks and broke it, and gave it to them, saying, "This is my body given for you; do this in remembrance of me." In the same way, after the supper he took the cup, saying, "This cup is the new covenant in my blood, which is poured out for you."

This is a commandment from Jesus Himself to do in remembrance of Him. This is how we remember His sacrifice. This is how we remember the cross and the blood of Jesus that was shed; shed for our deliverance and healing so that we can have eternal life. We do this to remember his resurrection power and the power that lives on the inside of us. This is how we obtain intimacy with the Father.

Notice, the first definition speaks of exchanging intimate thoughts and feelings. The LORD longs for us to commune with Him, to communicate with Him, and to have relationship with Him; to remember His promises. Taking communion can heal! The Bread represents the body of Christ which gives new life and healing. The Blood is the foundation of the new covenant and His Blood makes us healed and whole. Do this often.

ASSIGNMENT

Get supplies to take communion today! Find some worship songs on the Blood of Jesus to play and meditate on. Search your heart that it may be found clean in the sight of the LORD. Confess and repent those things that don't belong and remove that which has built a wedge between you and Him. Take of it and remember Him. Keep your mind stayed on the things of God, throughout the day, as you worship and pray.

PRAYER

Jesus,

I thank you for your precious Blood. I thank you for the sacrifice you made on our behalf. I declare that, by your stripes, I am healed! I am whole! And I am set free, in Jesus mighty name. I draw closer and closer to you. I share my intimate thoughts and the deepest part of my heart with you, today. I praise you, Father, for all you have done and are doing in my life.

In Jesus Mighty Name, Amen

Day Ten **COMMUNION**

Luke 22: 19-20
And He took bread, gave thanks and broke it, and gave it to them, saying, "This is my body given for you; do this in remembrance of me." In the same way, after the supper he took the cup, saying, "This cup is the new covenant in my blood, which is poured out for you."

Day Eleven PRAY IN THE SPIRIT

If I could list one thing, I think every Christian should be skilled in, it would be praying in the Spirit! The Bible tells us that we are to pray in the Spirit, at all times. This is how we are able to tap into the perfect will of God.

Okay, I have to stop for a moment and be completely honest. Some days I have so much going on that it seems I can't even gather my thoughts together to really be effective in my prayer time. So, I have learned the art of praying in the Spirit BEFORE I start my day is my secret weapon! This has been, and continues to be, a complete GAME CHANGER for me; and it can be for you, too!

The Holy Spirit dwells and lives on the inside of you! He has His own prayer language; one that spills from your belly. We speak out by Faith and the Holy Spirit gives the utterance. Many times, I start to pray in the Spirit, but I don't 'feel' anything happening, or I may think to myself, "you sound silly", and I found myself questioning myself, "are you doing it right?" As I lean in and press on, in spite of myself, before I know it, the Holy Spirit begins to rise up in me and I feel the shift in my prayers. Sometimes, He will reveal exactly what I am praying; other times, I just pray and trust that, what was done in the supernatural realm, was the perfect will of the Father!

The main questions I get when it comes to praying in the Spirit is, "How do I know if I am doing it right?" or "How do I receive my prayer language?"

Let me address the first question: if you have been baptized in the Holy spirit and have received your prayer language, then you know you are doing it right; when you speak it out in Faith that the Holy Spirit, who lives on the inside of you, will, in fact, do as He says and utter the perfect will of God through you.

You may not feel like you are doing it right, but, if your trust is in the LORD and His Spirit, when you are obedient to HIM, allowing Him to have His way in your life, press past those thoughts of doubt and lean into Him then it will flow from you.

You may even notice a distinct shift at times in your prayer language by tone, sound, etc. as He utters things unto God. This can intensify as you press on.

With regard to the second question, "how do I receive my prayer language?": The Bible says that Jesus prayed to the Father, *asking* to send a Helper. Believers obtain the blessing of the Holy Spirit upon salvation but have yet to be 'baptized' in the Holy Spirit, which is a different experience.

When you pray and ask the LORD for the 'baptism' of the Holy Spirit, you receive it by Faith and you then couple your Faith with action, then begin to pray out loud. I always tell people to not pray using 'English' words. By Faith, you trust that the Holy Spirit is going to take over and begin to pray through you.

The Bible declares that, "**one who speaks in tongues speaks unto God.**' Your prayer language is something that builds up and edifies your Faith.

SCRIPTURE FOCUS
Jude 1:20 (NLT) But you, dear friends must build each other up in your most Holy Faith, pray in the power of the Holy Spirit.

So, today I encourage you to do this daily in your devotion time, throughout your day, and whenever you can. You will begin to see amazing results!

Praying in the Spirit is something that I have made part of my everyday lifestyle as a worshiper. I believe the Holy Spirit has prayed things through me that have completely aligned with the perfect will of God for my life. He is the only one who has the ability to pray things in the most perfect way. I trust that if the Bible tells me to pray in the Spirit at all times, then God must place a value on praying in the Spirit. So, I want to make sure that I am in alignment with His perfect will and my prayer language gives me the assurance that what is said is taking place in my life!

ASSIGNMENT
Get into the flow of praying in your prayer language every day. If speaking in your prayer language is new to you, then start by setting a goal; grab a timer, set it to five minutes, and begin to pray. Press In. For five whole minutes. As you grow in the things of God, so will your Faith and, as a result, the time you spend praying the perfect will of God will grow.

If you already pray in the Spirit on a regular basis, challenge yourself to believe and ask for new tongues, and to pray longer than you normally would.

PRAYER
Heavenly Father,

I thank you for the gift of praying in various kinds of tongues. I believe, today, that you are increasing my ability to pray in the Spirit. Do not let me go to sleep one more night without the ability to pray your perfect will on the earth, just as it is in Heaven. I decree and declare that I am a prayer warrior! I thank you that you have given me my prayer language and I will not forsake it. I will use it for your Glory from this day forward.

In Jesus Mighty Name, Amen

Day Eleven **PRAY IN THE SPIRIT**

Jude 1:20
But you, dear friends must build each other up in your most Holy Faith, pray in the power of the Holy Spirit

Day Twelve **HEART CHECK**

I Samuel 16:7 (NKJV) But the LORD said to Samuel, 'Do not look at his appearance or at his physical stature, because I have refused him'. For the LORD does not see as man sees; or man looks at the outward appearance, but the LORD looks at the heart.

Just as we sometimes go to the doctor for an examination of our physical body, likewise, we go to the King for an examination of the heart. It is not always fun to get or do an evaluation of the heart, but this is very necessary for all of us, so that God can get the most out of our lives, and we can be free of any hindrance and snare that might try to trip us up and prevent us from walking in our full potential.

Today, we are going to focus on these two mighty words, 'Heart Check'. What I mean by that is that we are not going to look at everyone else's wrongs, or pray for everyone else to be 'fixed, delivered, and restored'. Today, we are going to invite the Holy Spirit to help us search our OWN hearts.

As we have been going through these last couple of days getting closer to the LORD, maybe even using different tools to get the most out of our time with Him, I believe He is and will continue to stretch us. It is important for us to realize that it is OUR responsibility to do a HEART CHECK every now and then. If there is anything that lingers that does not belong, ask the LORD to remove it. If anything is weighing on you or pulling you away from your direct relationship to the King, release it and give it to Him. Let it be that, anything that builds a wedge between you and God, be removed. Do not let it stay. Resolve to let it be dissolved.

I remember several times in my life as I grew closer to the LORD, I really understood the power of my time of devotion and alone time with Him. I would feel the gentle nudge of the Holy Spirit to search my heart. So, I would pray Psalms 51, a very popular psalm that we all know, "create in me a clean heart, o LORD".

As I prayed, the Holy Spirit would bring to mind a person or bad habit that I was still clinging onto, maybe a flawed mindset I grew up with that He wanted to completely transform.
It was in those times the Holy Spirit was shedding light on and giving me an awareness of the issues, so I could release them to Him and be free from them.

I have to admit, it wasn't always the easiest thing to give these things up. There were times the Holy Spirit would bring things to me to address and I didn't feel like dealing with it or I didn't have a full desire to release it to Him yet. I wasn't ready, but I have learned to put my complete trust in the LORD. Deep inside, I knew, if He brought it to my attention, then He was ready to do the deep work of healing in my life with a purifying fire to purify that area in my life. As hard as it was, I invited Him to release it as I would continue to steward in prayer, every day, until I felt the fullness of release happen in my spirit.

SCRIPTURE FOCUS

Psalms 129:23-24 (KJV) Search me, o God, and know my heart: try me, and know my thoughts: And see if there be any wicked way in me and lead me in the way everlasting.

Let this scripture be your prayer for today and throughout the week until it becomes a regular occurrence for you to do a Heart Check. David writes, "search me, o God." He invites the LORD in to search His heart, to know the deep places of His heart. He goes on to say, "test me." That is a pretty fierce statement to make to the LORD! Not only asking to search his heart, but to also see every little thing, to test him, and lead him into all His ways.

Can I just be honest? I haven't always prayed this to the LORD; to ask Him to test me in areas in my life made me nervous! I believe the writer had such a deep trust in the LORD that he was OK with God testing him in these areas, because he knew that God was going to do it for his benefit and growth.

As you step into this assignment and pray to ask God to search your heart, I want you to know that the Father's love for you is so incredibly great that He will not put too much on you or give you more than you can bare. You may have old memories come up or things from the past come to mind that have haunted you up to this point. I encourage you to press in, rise above these moments, and continue to seek God's face. Press through and release those things to the LORD. Let Him purify you with His beautiful fire so that you can come out as pure gold!

ASSIGNMENT

Grab your prayer journal and pen, go to your quiet place, and sit before the LORD. Ask Him to search your heart and bring anything He wants to your attention. Declare, "Speak LORD, your servant is listening." As things come to mind, no matter how big or small, write them down and ask the LORD to help you release it completely.

PRAYER

Father,

Today, I pray that you would search my heart and see if there be anything in me that hinders, binds, or restricts your perfect will from operating in my life.

In Jesus Mighty Name, Amen

Day Twelve **HEART CHECK**

Psalms 129:23-24
Search me, o God, and know my heart: try me, and know my thoughts: And see if there be any wicked way in me and lead me in the way everlasting

Day Thirteen **NO SHAME**

I think it's perfectly fitting that today's topic is 'No Shame' after we just completed a Heart Check.

I'm just going to go ahead and expose the devil right now. One of the main tools he used against believers is shame, guilt, and condemnation. He has done this since the beginning of time! This is not a new tactic for him; he studies people and observes the best way to bring on an attack of shame, guilt, and condemnation seeking to devour God's people.

I also want to point out that not everything we go through in life can be contributed to the devil. A lot of times, it is our very own internal perspective of self-worth and how God sees us that contributes to further the cause of shame, guilt, and condemnation.

Shame, guilt, and condemnation can look different at times. It does not always look the same. I've seen this manifest in my own life. At times, I would do something that I'm not proud of like, maybe, I was too hard on my daughter about school. Later on, shame, guilt, and condemnation would try to hit my heart like an arrow, causing thoughts to surface over and over again about past mistakes and shortcomings.

Other times in my life, I have dealt with feeling shame about not praying or fasting enough; that my worship to the Father was somehow in lack. Whatever the case was, the enemy tried to use that to set up camp in my life, to try to control me and keep me down, so that I could not move forward in freedom and elevate in the things of God.

Sometimes shame and guilt can come from a family member or a friend in your life that is saying negative things to you. This cycle can become a very tormenting burden to carry. However, it may come so we need to have a Made-Up mind that it cannot and will not have a place in our lives anymore! Having been made whole in Christ, let's determine in our minds, right now, to shake off that lie of shame, guilt, and condemnation, <u>for good</u>!

The Bible says that the devil is the accuser of the brethren and he accuses us day and night. So, I challenge you to shut the mouth of the liar today! We can do that with the Belt of Truth, which is the word made flesh, King Jesus, and the sword of the Spirit, the Holy Spirit! It's important to note that you cannot use a tool if you are unfamiliar with it. You cannot use a sword without first learning and putting it into practice. You must first gain skill in that area.

It's time to renew our minds and saturate our hearts and spirits with the Word of God! Truth sets us free, period!

I hear the chains falling! There is power in the name of Jesus to break every chain, break every chain, break every chain!

SCRIPTURE FOCUS

Isaiah 54:4 (ESV) Fear not, for you will not be ashamed; be not confounded, for you will not be disgraced; for you will forget the shame of your youth, and the reproach of your widowhood you will remember no more.

John 3:17 (ESV) For God did not send his Son into the world to condemn the world, but in order that the world might be saved through Him.

And my personal favorite...
Romans 8:1 (ESV) There is therefore now no condemnation for those who are in Christ Jesus.

It is time to begin to meditate on the scriptures until they take root in your life. The word of God is a powerful tool to combat guilt, shame, and condemnation every day. I live in a place now in my life where I rarely have to cast down those mindsets, because I am constantly renewing my mind in the world and I am well aware of the enemy's tactics when he comes to me. I will say this, there are days that I have to put certain things under the blood of Jesus. I am so thankful that the LORD's Love, Mercy, and Grace have swallowed up a sea of guilt, shame, and condemnation forever more.

ASSIGNMENT

Think about the things in your life right now that may cause you to have feelings of shame, guilt, and condemnation; put each one of those things under the Blood today! Write them down and plead the Blood of Jesus over them; crumble them up and toss them into the trash as a prophetic act declaring, "It is OVER!"

PRAYER

Father,

I thank you for your Blood that set me free from all guilt, shame, and condemnation. I know that your word says that where the Spirit of the LORD is there is Liberty! I take hold of that Liberty of the Spirit, right now! I cast down all shame, guilt, and condemnation in every area of my life today. I will no longer be bound by these lies and I decree that whom the Son sets free is FREE INDEED!

In Jesus Mighty Name, Amen

Day Thirteen **NO SHAME**

Romans 8:1
There is therefore now no condemnation
for those who are in Christ Jesus

Day Fourteen A JESUS CENTERED LIFE

Most people want to know the key to a successful and fulfilled life. Well, I can tell you, without question, the key to success and fulfillment in your life, hands down, is a Jesus Centered Life!

Now, I know what some of you might be thinking, "I'm super busy every day and I try to do my best to put God first." I know, because I would say the same thing; but do you know what? There is a place in God that He wants you to THRIVE in! This is something that we must actively press towards every day! I don't want to just get by with only a few minutes a week in devotions or a nice Sunday service. Maybe donate a few cans of food to my local soup kitchen; oh no! What I want is more of Him!

I want my life to mirror what the Bible says it should look like; marked with signs, miracles, and wonders! I want to be so filled with the Holy Spirit that my shadow does most of the work for me as I keep my eyes on Jesus! He is our great example, the one we look up to! His life was completely sold out for God and centered around the Father! He never moved, unless His Father said move. He never spoke, unless His Father said speak, and He never healed, unless His Father said heal! He lived in complete obedience and submission unto God! 100% completely given over to God! So, when you do a 'Heart Check' and something comes to your attention that you should submit to God, do not hesitate! The Holy Spirit will guide you into ALL TRUTH and move you from Glory to Glory. You will LEVEL UP!

SCRIPTURE FOCUS

Matthew 6:33 (NIV) But seek first His kingdom and His righteousness, and all these things will be given to you as well.

Ask yourself, 'What is His Kingdom?' 'What is His Righteousness?' Think on these things.

II Chronicles 18:4 (NIV) But Jehoshaphat also said to the king of Israel, "First seek the counsel of the LORD.

In review, what situation were they facing at the time? How would seeking God first benefit them? Here is something I want to just lay before you and ponder over: Is Jesus at the center of your ENTIRE life? Today, He wants full ownership, not weekend visitation. He wants to be a part of your marriage, your job, your dreams, your free time, and so much more! Every day is an opportunity to give yourself to Jesus and present your body as a living sacrifice. Some days, it may be easy and other days may prove to be a challenge. If you purpose in your heart to have a Jesus centered life, you will see Him manifest in your everyday life.

ASSIGNMENT

Pray and ask God to reveal areas that you need to give to Him. Write them down and make a commitment to give those things over to God fully!

PRAYER

Father,

I praise you, because you love me, not just enough, but, more than enough, to draw me closer and closer into you. Today, I give every single area of my life over to you. I invite you and give you permission to have your way. If there be any place in my heart and life that is not fully surrendered, please reveal them now.

In Jesus Mighty Name, Amen

Day Fourteen **A JESUS CENTERED LIFE**

Matthew 6:33
But seek first His kingdom and His righteousness, and all these things will be given to you as well

Day Fifteen **DESIRE**

de-sire –verb
1. *to wish or long for; crave or want.*
2. *To express a wish to obtain, ask for or request*

God wants us to have such a great desire for Him that everything else pales in comparison. Meditate on the definition and reflect on how you see God. Is there a strong feeling of wanting Him more? Some find they have a strong desire for the LORD to live their lives to please Him and others fade away until His voice is the only voice that matters!

If you are saying to yourself you would like that, but you don't think you are quite there yet, then you're at the perfect place of seeing that spark turn into a burning flame, an all-consuming fire! Don't get discouraged if you are not yet where you want to be. The fact that you want more is just confirmation that the LORD has placed a desire within your heart, and He will see it through to completion!

Below are three things you can do to increase your desire for the things of God and for the LORD:

① Pray Into It - Don't just wait to see if your desire increases all on its own, if you aren't intentional about it most likely it won't happen. In your daily prayer, ask the LORD to increase your desire for Him and to give you the desires of your heart (placing those desires in you). I pray this constantly, even if I see my desire increase, I pray for even more and the LORD said, "if we ask, we shall receive."

② Stir It Up – if you think on something over and over, it becomes even bigger in your heart and mind. This goes for something negative or something positive. Stir up desire by reading about Jesus, His glory, His character, moves of His spirit and His Love. Sing about Him; increasing your desire and begin to stir it up!!

③ Take Action – "Faith without works is dead," the bible says. We can step out and take action when it comes to increasing our desire. If I desire to see the healing hand of God in my life, I will pray into it, stir my faith in that area by reading scriptures on it, mediating on it; then I may take an action by traveling to a healing ministry or taking an e-course on it or getting some resources that will continue to challenge me in that area, until see the full manifestation of it in my life.

SCRIPTURE FOCUS

1 Kings 9 (NIV) When Solomon had finished building the temple of the LORD and the royal palace, and had achieved all he had desired to do, the LORD appeared to him a second time Solomon had a desire to seek the LORD more and to do something in honor and reverence for His LORD.

We see here that after he did what he desired in his heart, *immediately* the LORD stepped on the scene and met him AGAIN! The LORD is drawn by your desire for Him.

The psalmist David describes his desire and yearning like a deer that pants for the water. Oh LORD, give us that kind of deep desire for you and we know you will take us to the next level!!

ASSIGNMENT

Pray into this every day! **STIR IT UP. TAKE ACTION!**

PRAYER

Father,

I truly yearn for you. I ask that you increase my desire to pursue your heart with reckless abandon. I want to be set ablaze by your presence and live in such a way that it pleases you. Remove anything in me that doesn't please you. Get me to a place of Glory where you can dwell; move and be as you are.

In Jesus Mighty Name, Amen

Day Fifteen DESIRE

1 Kings 9
When Solomon had finished building the temple of the LORD and the royal palace, and had achieved all he had desired to do, the LORD appeared to him a second time Solomon had a desire to seek the LORD more and to do something in honor and reverence for His LORD

Day Sixteen **OIL UP**

In this season, it's so important that we realize the importance of being filled with oil, meaning being filled with the Holy Spirit. So many people today are living a Christian life void of the Holy Spirit. The reason that I know that they have a void of the precious Holy Spirit is because you don't see the fruit or even the character of the spirit of the living God in their life. You don't see the gifts of the spirit activated. You don't see the fruit of the spirit activated and that is a clear sign that there's a major problem. Most of the time, you will notice these people have deep religious mindsets, are very rigid, and harsh in their thinking and their reactions and interactions with people can be very negative.

We know that in the Bible, it uses oil as a symbol of the infilling of the Holy Spirit. David even writes in *Psalm 23*; He says, *"you anoint my head with oil and my cup runs over."* God wants us to overflow with His precious spirit.

You cannot just rely on a good Sunday service with a few great songs to get you through the week. We desperately need the Holy Spirit actively bringing truth to every area of our lives.

You're taking this 21-Day Life study course, because you have a desire to go up to the next level and God. I'm here to tell you today that you need to be overflowing with the Holy Spirit to go from glory to glory. His spirit is shown in the Bible in many symbolic ways: oil, a dove, fire, wine, and even fragrance, but please know that the Holy Spirit is a person and this person wants to live in you completely and fully. He is going to reveal Jesus and the Jesus reveals the Father.

SCRIPTURE FOCUS

Matthew 25:4 (NIV) The wise ones, however, took oil in jars along with their lamps.

Wise people know the importance of continual fellowship with the Holy Spirit. It's so important to make an intentional acknowledgement of the Holy Spirit EVERY. SINGLE. DAY. I can't imagine ignoring the Spirit of God that was sent to lead and guide me in all Truth. The one that comforts me is my advocate. He helps me and refreshes me. As we are talking about this, if you find that you have possibly done this or are doing this now, simply repent and come back to Him. Ask God to forgive you and move forward in Peace. We can ask for a fresh filling from the Holy Spirit, anytime. He is not selfish and gives it freely! He desires to be with you. He calls you His!

What are you waiting for? Get your cup and get filled up! It's time to Oil Up!

ASSIGNMENT

Ask for a fresh infilling today! Get ready for new tongues, Peace like a river, and even a word from the LORD. Sit and write down areas where you feel you need more Oil. Pray and Invite the Holy Spirit into those areas.

PRAYER

Father,

I thank you for giving me your precious Holy Spirit to lead me and guide me that I may truly know what your Holy Truth really is. I ask you today to fill me up; may my cup never run dry. Refresh my spirit and soul. Father, make my cup overflow with the oil of your Spirit, today and every day.

In Jesus Mighty Name, Amen

Day Sixteen **OIL UP**

Matthew 25:4
The <u>wise</u> ones, however, took oil in jars along with their lamps

Day Seventeen YOUR TONGUE

Okay, family meeting time! Let's talk about the tongue today! You want to level up and go deeper in your walk with the LORD? Walk in Purpose? If you truly want to grab a hold of all of these things, then we must have a chat about the words you choose to let leave your mouth gate, how you 'un-filter' the very breath of God within you, and how your words can send you down a path of failure or success.

We've heard it before, 'Life and Death by the power of the Tongue', but has this message taken root within your heart? I ask because, if you truly believe the Word of God and what He says about it, then you would probably be full of wisdom, guard your hearts ferociously, and watch every word that comes out of your mouth, right? I have had to catch myself at times and retract many a statement that I have made; mostly, out of a state of frustration through casual conversation. I realized my proclamation DID NOT line up with the Word of God and, if I did not counter this with repentance, it could affect situations in my life and/or the life of others. I used to say things like, "I'm so tired, I'll probably end up sick" or "I'm going to lose my job" or "my marriage was over." These things were NOT life-giving words; they were words of death.

Taking just this one statement, "I AM" as an example. When we speak "I AM", we must remember who "I AM" is! When we say, "I am this" or "I am that" our words are declaring who the Great I AM is and we know He is not sick, or tired, or going to lose His job, right? Sounds silly, but, in short, we declare who we are by declaring who God is. So, I challenge you to remember who I AM is the next time you say, "I AM this or I AM that". Renew your mind and replace your statement with, "God (I AM) is this or God (I AM) is that" or "I AM the daughter of the King, I AM a child of the Most-High God," etc. If your statement does not line up with the Word of God, then never let it leave your lips! In fact, take the thought captive, rebuke the enemy, and replace your statement with something that lines up with the Word of God. We are made in His likeness, so ask yourself, do you know who I AM is?

I took the LORD at His Word. I determined in my heart to be wise about my words and to strategically confess things that would bring life to a situation, instead of death and lies.

I began to say, "My Marriage is whole and healed, in the name of Jesus!" I began to say (even if I may not have seen it yet), "I have more than enough, and I AM more than enough!" After time, I would see these things come to pass.

This is the Word of God for you, today – **WATCH YOUR MOUTH!!**

Now with that being said, let's dive into some scriptures today and ask the Holy Spirit to reveal to us His heart concerning this....

SCRIPTURE FOCUS

James 3:5 (NIV) Likewise, the tongue is a small part of the body, but it makes great boasts. Consider what a great forest is set on fire by a small spark. The tongue also is a fire, a world of evil among the parts of the body. It corrupts the whole body, sets the whole course of one's life on fire, and is itself set on fire by hell.'

James 3:9-11 (NIV) With the tongue we praise out LORD and Father, and with it we curse human beings, who have been made in God's likeness. Out of the same mouth come praise and cursing. My brothers and sisters, this should not be. Can both fresh water and saltwater flow from the same spring? My brothers and sisters, can a fig tree bear olives, or a grapevine bear figs? Neither can a salt spring produce fresh water.

Psalms 37:30 (NIV) The mouths of the righteous utter wisdom, and their tongues speak what is just.

Proverbs 18:21 (NIV) The tongue has the power of life and death, and those who love it will eat fruit.

Deuteronomy 30:19 (NIV) This day I call the heavens and the earth as witnesses against you that I have set before you, life and death, blessings and curses. Now choose life, so that you and your children may live.

I must say, those are very powerful verses and, not only encourage us to speak Life and be wise, but they also warn us about being careful with our words. Today is the day for a radical change in how you speak. Think about what you are saying over you, your children, marriage, finances, church leaders, nation, or situation. Most importantly, what is your declaration unto the LORD? Make up your mind today to start declaring life to all those areas and more, in Jesus name.

ASSIGNMENT

I declare life over my **(Make a list and say it out loud)**. If you say something negative don't beat yourself up, repent and be intentional. Change those words to **live-giving words**!

PRAYER

Father,

Today, I choose life and commit to no longer coming into agreement with the enemy and his lies. I decree I am wholly healed and set free and the Spirit of the Almighty God is living on the inside of me. Everything I thought will prosper.

In Jesus Mighty Name, Amen

Day Seventeen YOUR TONGUE

Proverbs 18:21
The tongue has the power of life and death,
and those who love it will eat fruit

Day Eighteen **A TIME TO SUBMIT**

I remember when I thought 'submit' was a bad word! I had a lot of emotional and spiritual healing to go through. To me, fully trusting anyone, including my husband or leaders, enough to submit to them was a huge challenge for me. I was taught a false doctrine that submission means slavery and that is just simply not the case.

In the Kingdom of God, we can find great freedom in first submitting to God and also submitting to one another in Love. Let's break this thing open today and gain some truth on the subject of submission.

Jesus lived a life of submission to His Father; this He did by choice! I have found in my life that submitting to others is almost impossible, if you haven't first yielded submission to God and all His ways. So many people struggle in this area but understand that submission is not a license to be oppressed or abused by anyone; this is NOT the heart of the Father. Keep in mind that He FREED the Jews from slavery, not the other way around. It can prove challenging in our flesh to yield to the will of another. Keep in mind, man can fail us, but God IS NOT MAN! He comes so that we may have life and have it more abundantly. Yielding to God comes with Trust. We must leap towards a trusting relationship with God and know He will not tell you to do something if it would harm you in any way.

To get to the next level in this, it will need to be something that is fruitful in your life! I submit (yield to and deeply respect) my husband, because I TRUST HIM. I submit to my fellow brothers and sisters in Christ, because I prefer others over myself and I don't always have to have my way. This didn't happen overnight, but through a process of restoration and revelation of the Word of the Father in my life.

Here are some areas I want you to think about, to really do a "Heart Check" on, and determine to resolve if you have submitted fully to Gods desire.

Examine your Heart in these areas and <u>Submit yourself unto God:</u>

- **Your Spouse**
- **One Another**
- **Spiritual Leaders**
- **Authority at Work**
- **Governmental Authority**
- **Stewardship**
- **Tithes and Offerings**
- **Praying over Leaders**
- **Spending Time in the Word**
- **Prayer and Worship**
- **Your Tongue**
- **Your Plans**
- **Not Always Getting Your Way**
- **Your Holy Temple**
- **Your Mind, Will, & Emotions**
- **Your Worship**

Well, how did you do? If we are honest, there is at least ONE or more areas we could improve on, right? Let's take these things to the LORD. Once I began to desire God's will over my life and, out of obedience, humble myself in these areas, I began to see incredible results! And, you will too...

SCRIPTURE FOCUS

Hebrews 13:17 (NIV) Have confidence in your leaders and submit to their authority, because they keep watch over you as those who must give an account. Do this that their word will be a joy, not a burden, for that would be of no benefit to you.

James 4:7 (NIV) Submit yourselves, then to God. Resist the devil, and he will flee from you.

Ephesians 5:22 (NIV) Wives, submit yourselves to your husbands as you do to the LORD.

ASSIGNMENT

Search out two or more scriptures on the topic of submission and meditate on them. Pray and ask God to forgive you in any area you have not been in Holy Submission unto Him and begin to hand it over to Him in prayer.

PRAYER

Father,

I thank you that you are bringing me into a greater revelation about submission. I give you permission to tear down and rip up all the lies the enemy has tried to plant in my heart about this and let your Truth set me free, THIS DAY! I submit to you, Father. Teach me how to line up with your word and submit to others in every way you see fit and in all other areas,

                          In Jesus Mighty Name, Amen

Day Eighteen A TIME TO SUBMIT

James 4:7
Submit yourselves, then to God.
Resist the devil, and he will flee from you

Day Nineteen THE CHILDREN'S BREAD

Deliverance is the children's bread! Before I can dive into this, we need to look at Matthew 15: 22-28 to first understand where this saying came from.

Matthew 15: 22-28 (NIV) A Canaanite woman from that vicinity came to him, crying out, "LORD, Son of David, have mercy on me! My daughter is demon-possessed and suffering terribly. Jesus did not answer a word. So, his disciples came to Him and urged Him, "send her away, for she keeps crying out after us. He answered, "I was sent only to the lost sheep of Israel." The woman came and knelt before Him. "LORD, help me!" she said. He replied, "It is not right to take the children's bread and toss it to the dogs." Yes, it is LORD," she said. "Even the dogs eat the crumbs that fall from the master's table." Then Jesus said to her, "Woman, you have great Faith! Your request is granted." And her daughter was healed at that moment.

Many of you know my story about being saved and even being on the worship team at church, but I went through a fierce deliverance. I truly believe many people in the church need a good dose of the delivering power of Jesus, but Satan loved to feed them the lie that Christians don't need deliverance; that there is no way they can be oppressed by evil spirits. Well, I don't know what world they live in, but, as I travel the country and beyond, I see people continually getting set free EVERY. SINGLE. TIME from the demonic realm. Deliverance is what Jesus calls 'the Children's bread." Not the unbeliever's bread, but, rather, a blessing for God's children. Deliverance is needed to get to that next level in God.

I had bitter roots of unforgiveness, hate, rebellion, rage, rejection, fear, witchcraft, and a spirit of heaviness in my life. One day, during a church service, I was radically set free and that's the point when my worship life took flight off to places that I never knew existed! I was free and free indeed!

I want you to start believing God to deliver every wrong mindset, stronghold, hindrance, or chain in your life that could be hidden, or you were just unaware of. Ask God to expose it and bring it to light. Ask Him to walk you through the deliverance process.

You may need to renounce some things and/or repent along with telling the devil to GO! You can see deliverance in your teens, your marriage, your job, and every area of your life. Our God is Mighty to Save!

JW ACADEMY MEMBERS ONLY
There are Audio Prayers on Deliverance. You will find these in the "Prayer Wall" section of the JW Online Academy in Teachable.

SCRIPTURE FOCUS

Genesis 49:18 (NIV) I look for your deliverance, LORD.

Exodus 14:13 (NIV) Moses answered the people "Do not be afraid. Stand firm and you will see the deliverance the LORD will bring you today."

Romans 7:25 (NIV) Thanks be to God, who delivers me through Jesus Christ our LORD!

ASSIGNMENT

Write out areas you may need deliverance and go after it in the Spirit. Go to YouTube and find the audio called, "Prayers that Rout Demons' from Apostle John Eckhardt. Do a 'Heart Check' and, if there is anything you find outside of the will of God, give it to Him in prayer.

PRAYER

Father,

I come to you and give you permission to search my heart. Deliver me of anything that is not from you; religious thinking, strongholds, all chains that have me bound, or demonic influence that I might have been subject to unaware. Deliver me right now, in the name of Jesus. I don't want to wait another minute to be closer to you. Draw me in and hide me back under the Wing of the Almighty where I am safe in you. I know you have paid a hefty price so that I may be set free. I declare that I am free indeed! I receive healing and deliverance for myself and my family.

In Jesus Mighty Name, Amen

Day Nineteen THE CHILDREN'S BREAD

Romans 7:25
Thanks be to God, who delivers me through Jesus Christ our LORD!

Day Twenty **COME UP**

Here we are at DAY 20! Time flies by when you're leaning into the things of God, growing and being transformed. I find myself using the words "Level Up" quite frequently. I get this saying from the Book of Revelation where John is taken up into the Heavens by the Spirit of God and sees an open door into the Heavens; he then hears a voice calling out to him to 'Come Up'. This is interesting, because he was already 'up', so to speak. He was in the Heavens and caught up by the Spirit of God, but he still had opportunity to continue to 'Level Up', as seen here in the fourth chapter of Revelation.

The Bible talks about going from Glory to Glory. Be mindful to never get so comfortable and complacent in the things of God that you no longer yearn for more. Do not become 'OK' with just settling for 'church as usual' or the 'regular Christian life'. Dare I say, commit to pursue the unusual and perfect things of God. John chose to listen to the voice that said, 'come up' and he saw things that were absolutely incredible, filled with wonder, and the majestic beauty of the Kingdom of God. He could have been okay with just simply being in the Heavens, but no, he wanted to see more!

Your attendance for this course is proof that your desire for more is there as well! You have made it this far and will continue to go farther in the things of God. God will meet your desire and do exceedingly abundantly above all you could ever ask or think! You are an amazing child of God and He wants nothing short of the best for you! So, the invitation to 'Come Up', or 'Level Up', still stands strong, today and every day!

SCRIPTURE FOCUS

Revelation 4:1 (NIV) After this I looked, and there before me was a door standing open in Heaven. And the voice I had first heard speaking to me like a trumpet said, "Come up here", and I will show you what must take place after this.

ASSIGNMENT

Take some time to rest and reflect on all that God is doing in your life. Journal your Final Thoughts and any progress you have made.

PRAYER

Father,

I give you praise for all you have done and all you are about to do in my life. We declare you are Holy and no spirit, but the Holy Spirit, is allowed in this place. We accept your invitation to "Come Up" higher to join and sup with you. I shake off all the things that want to drive a wedge between me and you or to pull me down and stop me from going to the next Level with you. I run to you, Father, and you see me from a far off.

In Jesus Mighty Name, Amen

… Day Twenty **COME UP**

Level Up

Romans 7:25
Thanks be to God, who delivers me through Jesus Christ our LORD!

Final Thoughts **REST & REFLECT**

Take some time today to simply just rest under the wing of the Almighty and reflect on all that we have learned during our time together in these last 20 days and the value that you took away from this experience. Listen to your favorite worship music and be an atmosphere changer. Write some reflections down and meditate on your favorite scriptures. Rest in His presence and find Joy in His words, for your Heavenly Father loves and adores you. Let the LORD sing His song over you today.

Remember to know who you are and whose you are; reflect on who I AM is! Take captive every thought from the enemy and never allow it to stay. Get rid of the remnant in your mind and remove the ashes of the old man. Remember to always accept the invitation of the LORD. Don't just invite the Holy Spirit into the room, rather, give Him the room. The room to work in your heart and life. Remember to search your heart and do a "Heart Check" in all areas of your life and do it frequently. Take time to always listen for a response from the LORD and hide the Word of God deep within your heart. Let the Holy Spirit take root and allow Him to uproot the enemy. Refuse to believe the lies of the great oppressor and live in total victory in Him. Give him your best battle cry and declare you are happy, healthy and whole, in Jesus Mighty Name.

I have greatly enjoyed our time together during these last 20 days. I encourage you to continue on in learning the things of God. I look forward to seeing you next month as we continue on learning and growing together!

Be Blessed, for there is a savior who gave his life so that you may be free!!

Books By Jenny

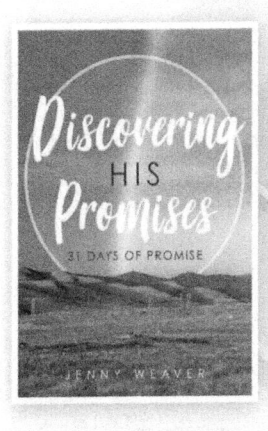

- Discovering His Promises: 31 Days of Promise
- Fear is a Liar: Overcoming Fear & Anxiety
- Resetting My Prayer Life
- the Sound of Freedom: How to Bring the God of Breakthrough into Your Toughest Struggles (Foreword by John Eckhardt)
- Daughter of the King Devotional Journal: Strong, Fearless, Beautiful

For more info, visit
JennyWeaverWorships.com

Made in the USA
Columbia, SC
23 May 2021